MEDICINE FOR THE
Youthful Mind

MEDICINE FOR THE
Youthful Mind

A Motivational Book for Teenagers and Young Adults

Tola Adeliyi

Library of Congress Control Number:		2012907889
ISBN:	Hardcover	978-1-4771-0666-2
	Softcover	978-1-4771-0665-5
	Ebook	978-1-4771-0667-9

This book was printed in the United States of America.

To order additional copies of this book, contact:
Xlibris Corporation
0-800-644-6988
www.xlibrispublishing.co.uk
Orders@xlibrispublishing.co.uk
300559

TABLE OF CONTENTS

DEDICATION

My Mother, Josephine Adeliyi a symbol of Humility, Love and Faithfulness. She showers me with limitless love.

And

My late father, Chief Olatoye Adeliyi, my teacher, devoted friend, mentor, hero and my greatest cheerleader. You were the true epitome of success. Selfless, brave, inspiring, understanding and always giving. Always nudging me to strive for excellence. In life you towered above all, yet you were humble. In death you live on continually. You have truly left your giant footprints on the sands of time and will be alive forever! Sleep well beloved father, the great scholar!

And to

God, the source of all inspiration.

High Praise *for Medicine for the youthful mind*

❝ As a Pastoral Manager with many years' experience of working with teenagers, I know that this handbook can be used to provide motivation to so many students who currently suffer from low self-esteem and as a result do not achieve their full potential. *Medicine for the youthful mind* is written in such a captivating manner which enables the reader to believe anything is possible" *Angela Duffin (Veteran Pastoral Manager, Milton Keynes)*

"This book is not only fascinating but captures the truth of the human spirit. The rich experience of the author has informed illustrations in the book and made it very practical and easy to relate to. Many of us have reasons to justify failure and the content of chapter three in particular fights this deception in human perception. This book should not only be read by you, but shared with friends and family." *Kojo Wood, CEO, Enterprise Foundation International, London.*

"Information can be a powerful tool when put into action. This book is full of information and keen insights that will help to move you to a new level in your thinking. I suggest that you apply the principles you learn and make your dreams come true" *Trudy White (Youth Impact Coach, London)*

"Mr Adeliyi is to me and my colleagues a powerful symbol of inspiration. His commitment to our success is remarkable. The book is one of such commitments. Buy, read and tell others about it."—Ella Hill (Former Student)

"I have really benefitted greatly by being in Mr Adeliyi's lessons. Not only does he teach us in ways that made us easily recall, he is fun and a great source of inspiration to us. With this book you have the same opportunity of benefiting from the same wisdom that has helped me greatly. Great book!"—Rachel Pears (Current year 8 Student)

"I first met the author at a Parents' teachers meeting and what a positive impression he made on me. Like him, his book is full of inspiration both for the youth and parents as well. It has been said that 'The mediocre teacher tells. The good teacher explains. The great teacher demonstrates. The superior teacher inspires.' This is a book from a superior teacher that truly inspires" *Caroline McCluskey (Parent, Milton Keynes)*

Acknowledgement

I wish to acknowledge the invaluable help of the following people, who have not only contributed to the successful completion of this book, but also to my life as a whole.

My mother: Ever supportive of my dreams and aspirations. Thanks a million times!

My Sisters, Funlola, Ronke, Ranmi, Sunmola, Fisola, Damisi and Dayo and their spouses. My brothers Damilohun, Fisayo and Tomiwa and their spouses. Thanks for your support.

Engineer Isaac Haastrup and Dr. Segun Osinubi thanks for being there every time and all the time!

Jim Rohn (now late) and Les Brown, the best! True motivators. You taught me through your messages some of the most vital lessons in life. And I became an embodiment of your messages. Thanks for being the finest mentors anyone could wish for.

Tom Wood—Thanks for your passionate training tips from the *duplicator*.

To all my students past and present, my current KS3, 4 and 5 students especially year 8 and 9 set 2. Your confidence in me inspires me. Are there happier and more progressive students anywhere in the world? What could

I have done without you guys? My old tutor group 8GTA, (Stantonbury Campus), and my lovely tutor group, 7D3.

Lara Oguntoyinbo, for the encouragement and help with the first round of proof-reading.

To Anthonia Christopher, thanks for being there all the time.

Sofia Cox for taking time out of her busy schedule to read through my manuscript and for your constructive advice.

Danny Hayles, thanks for doing so much in so little time and for the wonderful illustrations.

Oluwabonilarajuasolo, Oluwakanyinsolami, and Karis. Precious jewels. Thanks for believing in me! And to Ewa, ever there! You have been by far God's greatest gift to me. Thanks for sticking closer than a brother!

Above all, the sacrifices and praises of my heart and lips go to God, the plenipotentiary, for His grace has made it all come true!

Foreword

by Mark Bennison

Tola is passionate about his work; and his work, in all its guises, is to inspire that same passion in others. This he does with aplomb. His is an approach to working with and to leading others that is steeped in integrity. He believes in the power of the individual to make a difference; in their own lives and in the lives of others and he himself lives by this belief.

Tola is a compelling communicator and both the young and not so young, hang on his words and are moved by his example. In our high school of over 1300 students and close to 200 staff, there will be very few who are not aware of his presence and his positive impact.

This book strikes a chord and in my view is very timely. Young people are coming into the adult world facing ever-increasing challenges ahead. The exponential pace of change in the world of work and the economy, in education, in global shifts of influence, in technology and the environment require the next generation to be both enterprising and entrepreneurial. They will need to become expert, lifelong learners. They will need to have the confidence to harness the prevalent and changing technologies. They will need to see themselves as connected global citizens, frequently reinventing themselves.

To thrive in this brave new world, young people, above all else, will need to be socially confident, articulate and self-aware. They will need to aspire higher and be driven to succeed. This book, which I can only recommend highly, offers highly intelligent reflection around all of these themes. In it, Tola presents a strong case for remaining positive and being proactive. He invites the reader to build dreams. And he offers creative strategies for their construction.

Mark A Bennison MA NPQH FRSA

Principal, The Hazeley Academy

Chapter 1

INTRODUCTION

"We only live once, but once is enough if we do it right. Live your life with class, dignity, and style so that an exclamation, rather than a question mark, signifies it!" Gary Ryan Blair

My life has been greatly enriched by reading many books. Some were not worth the time spent on them, but some have helped to give meaning to my existence and to make me more focused in my journey through life. I shall be grateful if these lines that I have written help students, teenagers, young adults, parents and anyone who might get to read this book!

I am convinced that you now hold in your hands a book that represents an influential force, and trust that you will be as serious about *reading* this book as I have been about writing it. It is my desire that these printed words will change into useful ideas and emotions that will become the tools with which to fashion a new path in life with new and worthy goals, and with a new determination to attain whatever good thing your heart desires. Most books are written to entertain or inform. This book is written to inspire you!

I hope that you will find this a *sincere* presentation of ideas that can bring value to your life. It has been said that sincerity is not the test of truth. It is possible to be sincere and be sincerely wrong. But I hope that you will find this book both a sincere and truthful presentation of life changing ideas.

Different people have different ideas about what they call success and what they call excellence. And that is understandable. Different people hold different things as important to them. However, whatever your measure of success is, it must be satisfying to you and must positively impact on society. There must be that sense of fulfilment and achievement.

How do we then define success. To many, success is about achieving a particular position in society, a good university degree, a remarkable title, an expensive car or a luxurious house. To others it is about having an outstanding business or ability to mingle with the "high and the mighty" in society. To some it is about the money.

While some or all the above mentioned achievements could be part of success, it's safe to say that we all know of people who can boast of having ticked some or all of the boxes mentioned above, but are in fact living empty, unhappy and unfulfilled lives. That would suggest that fame, fortune, power and other indicators of success which the majority of the world celebrates may not be true success. True success is much more than those.

To me, success is living one's life in excellence. It is having one's internal experience completely in harmony with one's external experience. I recently read an article by Darren Hardy in Success Magazine, and I really love the way he presented this truth. He talked about how those people who have achieved that external, material success will inevitably feel that something is amiss if they have not also acquired the thing that matters most. That which matters most he called *significance*. It is significance that allows the internal experience to be as beautiful as the external experience. Significance is about knowing that we have had a positive impact on others . . . . that our lives have been meaningful. The conversation shifts from one of power to one of *value*. He continued, "The interesting thing is that you can be 'successful' and not be significant, but you cannot be significant without being successful!"

If you are a student, a young adult or even a parent and you are at a point where you cannot truly say that you are satisfied with your life and your achievements then this book was written for you. Sit back and relax as you are about to uncover how to get on the road to success. Perhaps you have not yet reached your desired destination, but you know you are on the path that leads to that desired future. You will also find this book a useful guide.

The truth is, every one of us is on a journey in life, and in a few years or more we will all arrive at a destination. The big question is, where? What destination? The difference between where we arrive and where we wish to be will be based on what we are doing right or wrong today! Are your actions contributing to a successful future?

You see, failure is not a single storm of disaster that just blows upon you. People do not fail overnight. Failure is what we get for years of making bad choices. As one person aptly puts it, "Failure is the inevitable result of an *accumulation* of poor thinking and poor choices. To put it more simply, *failure is nothing more than a few errors in judgment repeated every day.*" *He continues,* "Why would someone make an error in judgment and then be so foolish as to *repeat* it every day? The answer is *because he or she does not think that it matters.* On their own, our daily acts do not seem that important. A minor oversight, a poor decision, or a wasted hour generally doesn't result in instant and measurable impact.

"It does not *seem* to matter. Those who smoke too much or drink too much go on making these poor choices year after year because it doesn't *seem* to matter. But the pain and regret of these errors in judgment have only been delayed for a future time! If at the end of the day when we made our first error in judgment the sky *had* fallen in on us, we undoubtedly would have taken immediate steps to ensure that the act would never be repeated again. Like the child who places his hand on a hot burner despite his parents' warnings, we would have had an instantaneous experience accompanying our error in judgment. Unfortunately, failure does not shout out its warnings as our parents once did."

It is therefore important to realise that the foundation for the next 10, 20 or 30 years is laid today! The time to fix the next 10 or 20 years is now! Twenty years from now you are likely to be more disappointed by the things you didn't do than by the ones you did do. So, it is time to move away from your comfort zones!

In order to have what other people do not have tomorrow, you must be willing to do what other people are not willing to do today. So this is truly about a few daily disciplines, which have the power to transform and change the course of your life forever. We shall discuss more about that in later pages of this book.

But right now, let us start with what we know to be true. Many people do not achieve what they are capable of in life, or what they have potential to achieve, rather, they operate within the context of how they see themselves. In plain terms people's success is not based on what they have the power to achieve, but what they believe they can achieve. "As a man thinks, so he is." So if you believe that you cannot amount to anything in life, then that is true. On the other hand, if you believe that you can achieve set goals, then that is also true for you. This means that you do not become what you want, you become what you are!

If you believe that you are useless and good for nothing, based on the messages that you grew up listening to, then you will likely end up being useless and good for nothing. The drive to get involved in activities that will transform your life will be lacking, hence little progress will be made in areas of life where it matters the most. My desire is that the messages in this book will interrupt the ideas you already have in your head about what your abilities are. So that you end up with a *"can do"*, rather than a *"can't do"* attitude!

The sky is the limit when you set your mind
on success!

In my experience as a motivational speaker, youth impact coach and as a classroom teacher, I realise that many of my mentees and students begin to do well as soon as expectations are raised. As soon as they are made to realise that they are better than they previously thought, they to try harder and harder and with a measure of success, they are encouraged to try even harder and achieve success they didn't think they could achieve! Confidence built is a life transformed!

Why do we have so many children with little confidence? Research has shown that often this is a result of the verbal information that some parents regularly feed their youngsters with. They talk them down and tell them they will never amount to anything. "A chip off the old block" they say and because their father was a failure, it must be genetic. Sometimes it is the attitudes that are projected onto children by parents or "role models"; Children therefore no longer know what they are worth! Past experiences, including parents' experiences have left them useless and see themselves less than they truly are, less than they are really worth!

It is therefore very necessary for you as a child never to allow the negative experiences of those you live with to rub off on you. Neither should parents encourage this negativity when they notice. Often, the excuse I hear is "that is the way he was born". A parent once told me 5 years ago that "he will never get better than a 'D' ". I asked her why she thought so. She sat me down and gave me a long explanation about the pattern that her son's life had taken and will always take.

She even told me that all her children are the same! I advised her to work together with me, so we could give her son a fresh start. We did, and the result was outstanding. In less than 18 months, her son was moved from the lower paper to higher paper. Eventually, he left the school with a B. The lesson there for me was that sometimes, there is conflicting information between home and the school. However, to get the best result from a child, the home must be very cooperative with the professionals in schools who are trained to help kids achieve their potential. In the same manner school must work with parents to bring out the best in a child. Parents should stop making excuses for their children; rather they should try to see how they can help them make progress. Johann Wolfgang von Goethe said "If I accept you as you are, I will make you worse; however if I treat you as though you are what you are capable of becoming, I help you become that"

Teachers should also be careful to not give up easily on children, as many of them can change for the better. We should not reinforce negativity or use words that the young and highly impressionable students will accept as true and have their futures affected by.

No one, I repeat, no one-student or parent, should allow the negative opinion of others to become their reality! If the school data says you can only achieve a D, it is your responsibility to strive to change that. It will not happen in a day. But if you are determined and work hard, you will achieve your aim. I have seen it happen over and over, and I am now convinced beyond reasonable doubt.

From a very young age you need to know that if you desire particular lifestyles, you need to do things in ways that are consistent with what your goals or desires are. You need to do certain things in a certain way to get certain results. Those results you get will be based on some consistent actions. The actions will be as a result of you having the right mental attitude about what you think is right and important.

In simple terms, you need to have the right philosophy (thinking, belief) in life from a young age. The first step towards changing your whole life is to change your mind set. Someone once defined insanity as doing the same thing repeatedly, but expecting a different result. You need to re-orientate and begin to work on yourself, on your mind! One of my mentors once said that better selling begins with a better you! That statement is true for all walks of life. A better student begins with a better you! A better teacher begins with a better you! That means that self-development is more important than whatever thing you do. Once you have worked on your mind and yourself, you will be a better student, marketer etc. In other words, you will excel because of the person you have become!

Chapter 2

DREAMS

"I have had dreams and I have had nightmares, but I have conquered my nightmares because of my dreams."—Jonas Salk

There are so many factors that can shape you as a child. We are shaped by the surroundings we live in, some environments support us well, some do not. Sometimes, it is the kind of parents you have, the type of career they have, type of schools you attend(ed) or the part of the world you grew up in. You can also be affected by events. Some are major setbacks, many are personal, like the death of a precious family member. Other times we may be affected by national occurrences beyond our control, like conflicts and wars or economic woes. These events can have a big impact on our lives, positively or negatively. However, none of these factors has as much potential power for affecting our futures as our ability to dream.

Whatever we do we must allow the tug or the pull of the future to be the most important pull in our lives. Powerful dreams have the ability to urge you forward, drawing you like a strong magnet. The stronger they are, the more they draw you forward. They can pull you through negative events and disasters. Some people do not recover from disasters because they have nothing to live for anymore. There is nothing on the other side to make life worth living. No dreams to look forward to!

Dreams are a projection of the kind of life you want to experience. Someone described dreams as adrenalin injections.

"They can make you skip over obstacles or walls that you never thought you could overcome. When you allow your mind to open up and your dreams to take wings, they can unleash a creative force that can overpower any obstacle in your path!"

Note that it is only dreams, and not wishful thinking, that have the potential to unleash this creative force. Clearly defined dreams! A dream that does not have a future would not have the creative inspiration or the pulling power to make things happen. Therefore to really achieve your dreams, to really have your future plans pull you forward, your dreams must be clear. Not fuzzy dreams or wishful thinking. Yes we all have nightmares and fears but let us conquer our nightmares with our dreams.

. . . . *Too Young to dream?*

Every time I have a new group of students, I always try and get to know them by asking them to share their dreams for the future with me. Only a few of them have a fuzzy idea of what they want to do in the future. Most could not be bothered. Then one boy said to me "Sir, but I am only 16!" By the time I was 16, I had wanted to be a principal, a teacher, an aeronautical engineer, a doctor, a lawyer and a business man! I remember growing up and seeing my father as he put on his beautiful suits, I wanted to be a principal of a big international school like him. I couldn't wait to grow up! No one could have offered suicide as an option to ease any life pain, as I was too busy trying to grow up and live my dreams. I looked forward to growing up because it meant living my dream. These dreams made me work harder, even though I kept changing the dream of what I wanted to become.

Now the big question: Is it too early for a 16 year old to dream? Or even a 10 year old? My dreams started long before I was 10, and I think the earlier we start to dream, the better it is for us and the more focused our lives will be. You should not only start dreaming from a young age, you should start asking teachers, parents or role models what you need to start doing to achieve that dream. What subjects you need to concentrate on! Most world achievers started dreaming and following their dreams very early on in life. Tiger Woods started playing golf at the age of two! The Williams sisters (Serena and Venus, former world number 1) started playing tennis at 5. Lewis Hamilton started racing remote controlled cars at 6 and started car racing at 8.

You have got to be a dreamer. You've got to see the future. You've got to see the finish line while you're running the race. You've got to hear the cheers when you're in the middle of an impossible task and you've got to be willing to put yourself through the paces of doing the uncomfortable until it becomes comfortable.

Oftentimes, when you begin to dream, there are voices that will remind you of how impossible your dreams are. Your best friend may be that voice! It could even be your parents or your teacher. You will hear warnings like "get real." I can imagine what critics and even friends must have told the Wright brothers (the inventors of the airplane) as they sought to turn their dreams of flying an object heavier than air into reality.

It has been said that where there is no vision, the people perish. However, I am amazed today at the number of people who sleep every evening and wake up every morning with no dreams or plan for their lives, long term or short term! Although when you ask them what they want to achieve in life, they often say they want to be successful. When you ask further; ". . . what would you like to be successful in?" You become like a barbarian to them.

They have no idea what you are talking about! As far as I am concerned, these people have resigned themselves to fate. They use the crossed finger theory of "whatever will be, will be."

If you desire success in any area of your life, you must begin to dream. Having a dream or vision is as important as the steps towards the realisation. For a man without a vision really does not have anything to live for.

On a Larry King Live show, Bill Gates, one of the richest men in the world was asked the reason behind his stupendous wealth. He replied that there are three factors responsible for his success.

1. Vision and dreams
2. He was in the right place at the right time
3. He took massive action.

Only the first element will be dealt with in this chapter.

All successful people I know and have studied have been men and women of vision. They "saw" long before they saw. That means they saw in their dreams before they saw in reality. Their dreams and visions were not fuzzy. They had the ability the "see" clearly what they wanted before it existed.

I recently read the story of Ray Kroc, founder of McDonalds as told by Wayne Berry. He had a vision of what McDonalds could be. He saw McDonalds as an international franchise operation dominating the world of fast food. He had that vision when he first met the McDonald brothers in Southern California. The McDonald brothers knew he was crazy right away. They just couldn't see it! They had actually tried franchising and failed. If Kroc was stupid enough to try again where they had failed, sure they would go along with him, and he could have a percentage of the new company. That percentage was eventually worth billions of dollars to Ray Kroc, who was not at all surprised when McDonalds succeeded on a scale that astounded the McDonald brothers.

Bill Gates could "see" that the future of computers was in the software, not in the hardware. In the 1950's Walt Disney "saw" a place called Disneyland where people would come from all over the world to play. He saw this in a world where amusement parks were messy places staffed by shabby people. The bankers Walt approached just couldn't see it! The project was said to be laughingly referred to as "Disney's folly", but Walt did it anyway!

I am sure we all know or have heard about one of the Disney Parks around the world. No one is laughing at Walt or his ideas anymore!

So what's your vision? What is it that you want to achieve in life? You need to first see in your mind's eye. That is the starting point. Your mental attitude must be brought in line with your vision. There must be a complete reorientation. If you desire a particular lifestyle, you need to do things in a certain and definitely different way to get the type of results you want. Those results will be directly related to the type of habits you have formed. Your habits are also a result of consistent actions. Your actions are a result of you having the right mental attitude about what you consider or believe to be right and important to you.

It has been said that if you plant a thought, you should harvest an action. If you plant an action, you will harvest habit. Plant a habit, and you will harvest your character. Plant a character and harvest a destiny. Many have sealed their destiny with negative thoughts that became actions, and actions that became habits, and habits that became their character, and the characters that sealed their destinies. How sad for those who did not realise that we are a result of everything we do!

Let our thinking pattern be more positive. The good news is the race of life is not ended yet. You can still live your dream and your dreams can still be achieved. Once you have the right mental attitude towards life, it will guide you to making quality decisions on how to plan your life and what philosophy you want to adopt in your everyday life, business and relationships.

We want to have success in every area of our lives, like we have never had before. We want to grow personally and eventually professionally in our journey to success, and we want to live with honesty while we achieve success and make money.

Your imagination is always the first step of the miracle of possibility. Reality starts with imagination. That elusive A*, or B or that new job is achievable! Reality starts with imagination. Imagine the possibilities. Then imagine that some of the possibilities are possible for *you!* What produces faith? Sometimes it is stories that demonstrate that your dream is possible and achievable. Dreams reassure our faith. I never cease to tell my students stories of how former students who were destined for failure turned their lot around. I do that because I know that for most, it generates faith; makes them believe that "if James can do it, then I can do it!" So keep reading and keep listening. What is possible for one is possible for another.

Lastly, you have to develop your faith into action, because affirmation without action is the beginning of self-delusion! I believe that we are all presented with many good ideas, some of these ideas may be ours or some may have been shared with us by friends. These ideas may have the potential to create bright futures for us. The problem is that most people, even when they recognise that they have a good idea, do nothing with it; unlike Bill Gates who took massive action instead of just talking about his dreams. It was Mario Cuomo who once said that there are two rules for being successful. One, figure out exactly what you want to do, and two, **DO IT!**

"Success never comes to look for you while you wait around. You have got to get up and work at your dreams to make them come true"—Poh Yu Khing.

I once told one of my students that I was impressed by the fact that unlike many, he had a dream, a vision of the future. However, I told him that he would impress me more when he had a plan laid out on how to achieve that dream and he is doing SOMETHING about it. Talk is cheap! Work hard at your dreams!

Chapter 3

Obstacles to Dreams

"Obstacles are those frightful things you see when you take your eyes off your goal."

-Henry Ford

Now let us play a little "game". Think about something you have thought about in the past few days, or few weeks or months or even years, that you know would bring value to your life, to your parents' lives or if you are a parent, to your children's lives and maybe to society at large. Usually, as soon as you start thinking of this great thing, some inner conversation will begin. These inner conversations are what I call the *dream thief.* This dream thief is the main reason behind your lack of achievement in the classroom, at work, at home or generally in life. Some examples of messages from the mind thief are:

- I am too short
- I am too fat
- I am too tall
- I am too dumb
- I have never done that before
- I am too old
- I am black
- No family member has ever done that before!
- No one loves me.

And the list goes on and on.

How many people have had plans to do something great, positive and meaningful and talked themselves out of it. I don't mean your parents or your friends. But you talked yourself out of it. It is this inner conversation, this dream thief, who always tells you that you are not capable of achieving anything in life. This inner conversation is the reason why so many people take their greatness to the grave!

Someone once said that the wealthiest place on the planet is not the gold mines of South Africa, or diamond fields or Hollywood. It is the **graveyard**!

There you will find all sorts. Great ideas that were never developed. Hopes and dreams that were never realised. You will find inventions that were never created and even songs that were never composed. Books that were never written and published. They were never completed because most people allow the inner conversation to take control. So, why do most people die with dreams and ideas?

1. Fear of failure:

It is a fact that men are born with two types of fears.

a.) The fear of falling and b.) The fear of a loud sound.

All other fears we learn, like the fear of spiders, fear of water and the fear of failure. Failure can be a friend or a foe. When people fail, they just give up or give in. However, great men look inwards and see where they went wrong and what they could have done to make it better. They do not stop there. They strategise, go back to the drawing board and try again even when they feel discriminated against. They bounce back, with vigour and more wisdom. Failure is nothing but an opportunity to begin again, in a more intelligent way.

I know many adults who would rather stay in the safety of poverty than venture out and risk the possibility of failing. You will sometimes fail many times on your way to success. My father used to tell me that in life, he would love me to be able to count my successes and count my failures, but never count the number of times that I didn't try.

Unfortunately, many teenagers seem to have the attitude of "I CAN'T." Even without trying, they have made up their minds that they cannot attempt that Science question, that Maths sum, that English activity. They have given up before they try. They are afraid of trying and failing. Remember, in the words of Walter Brunell, "Failure is the tuition you pay for success." By seeing the seeds of failure in every success, we remain humble and by seeing the seed of success in every failure we remain HOPEFUL!

The big question is how long should a child try walking before he stops trying and accepts failure? The answer is UNTIL he can walk! A kid doesn't stop trying to walk because it is difficult or because he has fallen down a few times. He or she keeps on trying UNTIL he or she succeeds.

2. People become comfortable with failure or the status quo.

After a measure of success has been achieved, or a level of "comfortable" poverty has been reached, many stop thinking of ways to improve. They become complacent and seem to accept their situation as the way it should be. I once read the story of a dog lying on the porch on a pile of nails, moaning and groaning. A passer-by asked why the dog was moaning. The dog's owner said it was because the dog was lying on a pile of nails and was therefore uncomfortable. "Why didn't he get up then?" asked the passer-by. "He is not hurting badly enough for him to get up". What an answer, and how that fits into many of our situations! People moan and groan about situations, about their homework, about friends. It would seem to me that they have the energy to complain, but not enough to do something about it.

It is amazing how many people are stuck in jobs they hate. They get paid enough so they don't quit and they work hard enough so they don't get fired. So they complain about their bosses, the environment and everything. And yet nothing is done about it. That is not how to live life.

I watched a TV programme recently where a lady was complaining about how life has been so unkind and how people have let her down. Complaining and moaning and groaning. "Why me?" she moaned. 80% of the audience don't really care! The remaining 20% are glad it is you and not them. Don't stay down, complaining about what they have done to you. Get away before they come back! Get up and move on with your life. Never be satisfied with anything but the best!

3. Where we are born/ background:

A lot of people are held back because of the circumstances that they found themselves in. Circumstances like where they were born, and their family history. Your history doesn't need to become your future. Mark Caine once said that the first step towards success is to refuse to be a captive of the environment in which you were born.

A student once told me "I am never going to be a graduate," I asked her why and she said that there were no graduates in her family. The father was a garbage collector and her mother was a dinner lady. I asked her what that had to do with her own dreams or the choices she has to make for herself. She looked at me and said nothing.

This girl is very intelligent, very academic, but with little confidence. I am sure it will be safe to say that she had no confidence at all. She never answers questions during lessons. But because we got on very well, she would ask questions after the lessons or during break. However, every time I asked questions she always replied "I know my answer is rubbish, but I think . . . ." Her "rubbish" answers were usually very correct and with a lot of depth. I realised that this was an extremely intelligent student with no confidence! She was much better than she thought she was. I needed to interrupt the messages in her head and in her mind. I needed to let her realise that her history, which has become her stumbling block, doesn't have to become her future reality. She started gaining confidence as I continuously assured her that she was much better than she thought she was. She ended up with a C in science, a grade that she never thought possible and obviously never achieved before. I wish I could have helped her achieve a B or an A, as I know very well she was capable of a grade B or higher.

It is not the circumstances that you find yourself in that defines the person you become; it is the personal choices you make. By the end of next year you and I would be the same person. The difference will be the choices that you and I make beginning from now till then. I therefore recommend you choose life and say YES to your dream and to a bright future.

I remember when I wanted to train to be a teacher. One of my friends advised me to sincerely reconsider my plan. They said they thought I had what it would take, and the experience necessary, BUT how could I teach English children when I came from a different background? In fact, one of them advised me to work at getting a license for driving the big garbage trucks because as he said "their pay is competitive". Don't get me wrong, there is nothing wrong with being a truck driver, if that was your dream and it would give you satisfaction for now and for the future. But that was not my dream. I love being a part of success stories and I would be able to do that in teaching. Another suggested that I should look for jobs in a good factory. My response to them was "what background knowledge would I use to deal with the foreman in the factories" His reply was "well, ok . . . true . . . ."

The reason for lack of good progress is not because we aim too high and we miss the target, it is because we aim too low and we hit the target! And then we convince ourselves that we are doing well! The affable actor, Will Smith, made a profound statement in his depiction of Chris Gardner's life, in the movie *the pursuit of Happyness*. He told his son; "don't ever let somebody tell you you can't do something. If you have a dream, you have got to protect it. People can't do something themselves, they want to tell you you can't do it. You want something, go get it. Period!" I followed my dream and the rest is history now.

Do not allow anyone to tell you what grades you can achieve or what your potential is! You must realise that people's opinion of you does not have to become your reality. I believe in revenge. And I don't mean "an eye for an eye" violent type of revenge, but like Frank Sinatra said, *"the best form of revenge is to be a massive success."* All those who believed you would never amount to anything, will all see and marvel at your success!

4. Excuses vs. Determination

One other reason people do not achieve their dreams is we often have too many excuses. We find it easier to blame our lack of success on everyone else but ourselves. You and I have probably heard every excuse under the sun.

   a.   No money
   b.   No time
   c.   I got sick

   d. I have a bad teacher
   e. No good friends
   f. No one likes my ideas
   g. They will laugh at me
   h. Circumstances beyond my control

And the list goes on!

The truth about you not having success yet goes beyond that. The truth is that you are your greatest enemy, not the man next door and not your teacher. Most of the time you fail because you failed and disappointed yourself. You promised yourself that you were going to do "something" and you never did, like study more, read more, reduce the time wasted on TV or be more serious with your homework. But you failed yourself. Yes, sometimes you may have the "bad luck" of having a "bad" teacher. Look beyond him or her and do not stress yourself out because of them There are many more teachers in that school who will help you if you find time to see them and seek for help. Your older sibling might even have more knowledge of a topic you would like to know more about. Ask him or her for help.

Follow your dream of achieving the grade you desire and are working towards. If you are thinking of ending up being fed by the government's welfare system, you may be disappointed. It is getting less and less lucrative. The British government is trying to get people out of the benefit system. It will be harder in the future!

Not doing what you promised yourself can be one good obstacle to our dreams. I am not talking about what your teacher, mentor or parents advised you to do, I am talking about what you promised yourself you would, and then failed to do.

I remember once I promised myself to stay away from unhealthy food. But over and over, until some years ago, I found myself doing just the opposite and convincing myself (and giving excuses) that just a bottle of fizzy drink would not kill me. I was thirsty and far from home. I am talking about the difference between being self-determined and **circumstantially determined**. When you are self-determined, you are determined no matter what the circumstances. But a circumstantially determined person is determined only when circumstances are favourable. And circumstances may never be favourable!

5. Not acting on Dreams:

One other big reason people never achieve their dreams is because they never acted on them. They have lofty ideas but they have no plans in reality to make this dream come true. Wayne Berry, one of the founders of the National Speakers association of Australia, put it in a way I would never have been able to.

"As one of the founders of the National Speakers Association of Australia (NSAA) 15 years ago, I'm sometimes asked if I'm concerned that I'm actually helping create competitors for myself, every time I speak at an NSAA conference or seminar. On these occasions I willingly share my knowledge and experience with people new to the speaking and training professions. I tell them what I've learned over the last 27 years and share ideas on how they can become professional speakers. Frankly, I'm not concerned at all about creating competitors, and I say this for two reasons.

"Reason number one is that I know that very few people will actually take action on the ideas I share. Not because they don't see the value in the ideas, but simply because that's human nature. They'll talk about doing something. They'll plan to do something. **But they won't actually do anything**. If they do, they'll only try it a time or two and if they haven't achieved overnight success then they'll stop doing it. The second reason I don't mind sharing my knowledge, is that I know that the serious people, the ones with vision who will take action, will not be interested in becoming Wayne Berry clones. They already have their own vision about what they want to become and achieve, and they'll do it too. They'll add real value in their own right in the marketplace. Every year I share ideas on selling and negotiating techniques with tens of thousands of sales people, but sadly only a small percentage will have the vision and the persistence to follow through and use these ideas on an on-going basis. Those who do, become enormously successful and send me emails which I really enjoy receiving."

"The real key to success is to find a good idea and take IMMEDIATE and MASSIVE action. You'll note that there are two factors here, IMMEDIATE and MASSIVE. My experience is that if we don't act on a good idea within 24 hours, we are less than 50% likely to ever act on it. If we haven't acted on it inside of 7 days, then we are less than 2% likely to ever act on it. My advice is when you find a good idea act on it right away. That way you'll find out quicker if it's a good idea or not. The other key is to take MASSIVE action. The average person will try a new idea once or twice and if they don't get an immediate result, they give up.

"The last time I was in Washington DC, I visited the Smithsonian Institution and saw some of Edison's failed experiments as he worked to perfect the incandescent light bulb. The problem was in the filament. They all burned out after a short time. Edison took massive action on the challenge and after thousands of failed attempts, he finally solved the problem. The solution made him a fortune. How is your MASSIVE 'persistence' factor when you are trying out a new idea? There is no such thing as I'll try and do it. You either do it or you don't!

Edison simply decided to do it, no matter what it took. Would you?

Chapter 4

Personal Development

"Excellence is never an accident. It is always the result of high intention, sincere effort, and intelligent execution; it represents the wise choice of many alternatives—it is choice and not chance that determines your destiny"—*Aristotle*

To become successful in whatever we do, we must change the way we think and the philosophy we uphold. You cannot be truly successful and happy without changing your outlook and refining the way you think. This book is not just about motivating people to act and do "stuff", it is about motivating someone with the right ideas and the right philosophy to act in ways that will help build a brilliant future.

If you motivate someone with a terrorist mind-set, he or she will be out in the street planting bombs and maiming innocent people. You have just developed a motivated terrorist. In the same way, when you motivate an idiot, all you get is a motivated idiot! If someone is going down the wrong road, he doesn't need motivation to speed him up. What he needs is education to turn him around and then motivation to get him acting positively. This is the purpose of that book!

That is the reason why we need truth to eradicate falsehood, and we need to replace gloom with hope. We need a different mind-set and productive values. To have more and achieve more, we need to know more and become more, and this is where personal development comes in. The first change is in our thought pattern; "As a man thinks, so he is!" It starts with the mind. But change we MUST, if we want to make a difference to our lives.

In my own experience, every single improvement came as a result of a change, changing something within me and modifying or getting rid of some negative habits. Not all changes result in improvement, but all improvements are a result of a meaningful change!

The most meaningful changes come from within. Unfortunately, the only person who welcomes change is a baby in wet diapers. For the rest of us, we don't want change! We are so set in our ways and most would stay in the safety of poverty or failure or even in the safety of our weak and beggarly existence than change! Until for some, the pain of remaining the same becomes greater than the pain of changing.

Nido Qubein once said that ". . . for the timid in society, change is always frightening. For the comfortable, change is always threatening. But for the confident amongst us change is opportunity." How true that is. This is because changes allow us to become the person who attracts success. Success is something you attract by the person you become.

My father always told me to work harder on developing myself than I work doing my job, and he also said that I should put in so much more in my job than I am paid to do. He said that if I am paid £10 for a job, I should put in £15 worth of labour. But he said I should work more on developing my mind than I do on the job! That way, he said, I will be building skills and stamina for my own future. I pass the same wisdom to you. Work harder on yourself, enhance your knowledge and become a better person. This is because only then does the marketplace appreciate you!

Study is part and parcel of your personal development, it activates the mind. I don't mean studying your Chemistry textbook alone. Yes, you must study your Chemistry books, but I am talking about what you do in addition to that. I am talking about reading books that will expand your mind. I am talking about being an independent and lifelong learner. Every outstanding person I know studies, every studious person eventually becomes outstanding, if knowledge they gained is applied. You cannot be a committed thinker if you don't study. You cannot think in a vacuum. You need to fill your minds with information! Good information. Otherwise, your mind will be filled with junk!

Isaac Newton, arguably one of the best scientists of all time, once said: "If I have seen further than others, it is by standing upon the shoulders of giants who have gone before me." He got inspiration from studying the work of great scientists who came before him. He studied the materials and improved on them. You will also get inspiration from the good books you read. You will get inspiration that will prepare you for a good future. People often say that what you don't know won't hurt you! On the contrary, what you don't know will hurt you. It will leave you ignorant and affect your achievement level. The books you do not read will not help you! What you don't know will hurt you and adversely affect your future. As someone once said "Ignorance is not bliss. Ignorance is poverty. Ignorance is devastation. Ignorance is tragedy. Ignorance is illness. Nourish the mind like you would your body, for the mind cannot survive on junk food."

Why do you need to prepare yourself? You need to prepare yourself because a great opening is going to show up in the future. When it does, what do you do? What do you do when opportunity presents itself? The only thing you need to do is to present skills, readiness and talent to opportunity.

You don't present needs to opportunity. It is better to be prepared and not have an opportunity, than to have an opportunity and not be ready! Everything you need to develop yourself is available! (within reading and listening reach.) But are you going to reach out and take advantage?

If you search you will find. Finding is reserved for the searcher. We don't find what we need; we find what we search for. Needing is not a condition for finding value. You cannot be a "needer," but a searcher. You don't just achieve a grade A, you must actively pursue the grade. You will not achieve grade A or B in your exam just because you need it. You must search actively for ways to achieve the grades you desire!

Part of personal development is the ability to work on our character. It is not enough to be knowledgeable and wise. It is not even enough to be a charismatic student or worker. Solid character must be developed, for character is what is left when charisma is gone!

Upgrade your mind and not just your face!

> "Beauty fades but dumb is forever!"

Character is not something you were born with and can't change. It is not like your fingerprints or the colour of your eyes. In fact, because you weren't born with it, it is something that you must take responsibility for creating. I don't believe that adversity necessarily builds character and I certainly don't think that success corrodes it. Character is built by how you respond to what happens in your life. It is about building the virtues of love, patience, gentleness, loyalty, faithfulness, kindness, empathy etc. The best approach to doing this is by putting yourself in other people's shoes. How would you feel if you were bullied? Not good I suppose, if so, don't do it to someone else! How do you feel when someone is patient with you and helpful to you? Great, I suppose. Then you have to treat others the same way! Whether it's winning or losing every game, getting rich or dealing with hard times, you must build character out of these qualities and diligently nurture them within yourself, just like you would plant and water a seed.

Note, that character is not how you act when people are around. It is not how you act when people you respect or those you would like to always see you in a good light are around. It is how you behave when no one is around. It is what you do, not because it feels good, but because you know it is right! It is what you do whether you are rewarded for it or not, whether anyone sees you or not. It may be as simple as turning off the lights in your classroom or helping to pick up litter from the floor, whether you put it there or not.

Since I started working in my current school, I have never left the light on in my classroom when I am not there. No one notices, but that doesn't matter. It is my little way of contributing to the environment and saving the school some money! I do it not because I want to receive a medal; I do it because it is right!

But do you want to know the really amazing thing about character? If you are sincerely committed to making yourself into the person you want to be, you'll not only create those qualities, but you'll continually strengthen them.

Parents have a lot to do with helping us with character. Recently we had a discussion about how much children have changed over the years. But if we take a closer look at the lack of character, you will discover that it is not children who have changed; it is parents. Parenting styles have changed over the years. Connie Podesta, an American psychologist shared her insight about character and parenting. 30 years ago she conducted a survey, in which she wanted to find out what parents wanted from their kids. 80% of the parents said they wanted their kids to be respectful, hardworking, resourceful and compassionate.

A few years ago she conducted a similar survey. This time their answers were that they wanted their kids to be happy. This is great, but happy instead of respectful, hardworking and compassionate? In trying to keep children happy, parents sometimes reinforce bad behaviours that eventually have a negative impact on the children. They make excuses for their bad behaviour, instead of correcting these errors. Some parents will not even allow their children to stay back for detention, if they misbehaved in school. They think they are doing the children a favour and keeping them happy! The kids may be happy in the present situation with their parents, but are they going to be able to cope with the ever increasing demands for excellence, strong character and the competition for jobs in the real world? With the type of excuses they are used to giving? I am not sure about that!

Chapter 5

SETTING GOALS

"Show me a clerk with goals and I will give you a man who will make history and give me a man without a goal and I will give you a store clerk"—J.C. Penney

I spoke to a parent of one of my students some time ago about the dangers of taking students on holiday during the school year. She explained why they had to take the time off, and what really impressed me was how well and carefully they had planned their holidays for 2009. This conversation was in January 2008. While I learnt something about how to plan my next holiday, I found it interesting that most people plan their vacations with better care than they plan their lives. Could this be because it is a form of escapism for some people? Getting out of misery for a few weeks, in a new environment and pretending that life is all good. In a few weeks we are back to the same old life! Perhaps that is because to escape is easier than to embark on changes that will positively impact on us on a daily basis.

If we can plan our lives as rigorously as we plan our holidays, we would all be better for it. If you don't carefully design your own life plan, it is highly possible that you will fall into someone else's plan. And guess what they may have planned for you? Not much.

It is therefore your responsibility to plan for your life as much as possible from a young age, setting goals for and mapping out plans to achieve them. How then do we define goals, and how are they different from dreams and wishes?

A goal is a *specific dream with a date or time in view*. Dreams are generalised, while goals are specific. They are also known as targets. Dreams are not so targeted. Wishes on the other hand are things we desire with no commitment towards them. Some wishes are just senseless fantasy and do not tend towards reality at all. But generally they are everything that you may need, want or desire someday, but that you are not actively pursuing at this time.

When I mentor students, I normally advise them to build their wish list first, and then prioritize and decide which of these wishes to pursue further. When you find a wish that you really want to accomplish, you simply convert it into a dream or goal.

Dreams can be big and seem unrealistic at first glance. They also don't have to be as focused or as specific as goals. Some dreams could be for five to ten years into your future; others could even span your entire lifetime. Dreams are your ultimate destination, while goals are the intermediate stops along the way. Dreams represent what you want and why, while goals represent your plan to get you there.

Goals and dreams complement each other. If you only dream without goals, you can easily feel discouraged by the size of your dream. The shorter-term goals provide achievable intermediate targets that serve as stepping stones towards your dream. If you only have goals but no dreams, you can easily run the risk of forgetting "why" you are pursuing these goals in the first place. Specific short-term goals are not really inspiring by themselves either; their power comes from their connection to a big inspiring dream.

In general, goals require more detail than dreams because they represent specific and focused targets. When a goal becomes unrealistic, it's no longer an effective goal. CHANGE IT! Bring the goal back into line with reality. You must be willing to adjust some features of the goal or change the time frame. I will give you an example:

When I decided to write this book 3 years ago, it was born out of a burning desire to inspire teenagers and young adults, beyond those I had contact with. I had no clear finishing date and I did not have a clearly defined plan. So, for one year all I achieved was completion of the first page. However, when in June, I worked out a strategy and set a finishing date, it was like magic. I identified all that needed to be done, people I needed to talk to and research that needed to be carried out. Then I had a setback. The document containing some chapters was corrupted for no apparent reason. I tried my best to recover and repair the file, all to no avail. I had to basically start all over. Even though I still tried to meet the deadline, when it was obvious that the former deadline was not realistic, I had to review the completion date. I changed it from the end of December to the end of January.

The skill of setting goals is a fantastic skill to develop, to give your life a purpose. A life best lived is a life by design; not by accident, not just 'winging it' and stumbling from wall to wall, hoping that things will fall into place. Goals must be SMART. SMART is an acronym used to describe "brilliant" goal statements. It stands for **S**pecific, **M**easurable, **A**ction-Oriented, **R**ealistic and **T**ime-Specific.

The best **SMART** goals are focused, specific, short-term targets that involve things that are mostly under your direct control. This is what makes goals such powerful tools for achievement.

Let us use a good example of how a goal should be set using "SMART" targets. Let us assume Paige, a year 12 girl, wants to set herself a target. If she says, I want to be successful in my exams, we would say that is a good way to think, but that is definitely not a smart goal! A smart goal would be:

> I want to achieve an "A*" in physics by the end of August (now that is **Specific**), when the goal is that specific you know clearly what you are working towards. Not only is A* specific, it is also **Measurable**, as you can understand the difference between grades A, B, C, D and E, you also know how many marks you need to achieve that. It is therefore easy to measure what type of progress she is making, if she is making any. Life expects us to make measurable progress in reasonable time.

If all she wanted was just to be successful, that would be difficult to measure. Moreover, many people have their own definition of success, so how do we measure success?

Now, every smart goal must also be **action oriented**. Paige must list certain action she needs to take to make this goal a reality. What person must she become to accomplish these goals? What would she need to give up? Maybe reduce time spent on Facebook for instance, in order to be able to spend more time exposing herself to past physics questions. Whose help would she need to enlist? She may need to get in touch with Mr William, her physics teacher, or enlist the help of a private teacher. There must be clearly defined actions geared towards her success in physics.

Another factor that needs to be considered is how **realistic** Paige's goal is within the timeframe given. If Paige has exams in January, and her predicted grade and best result in Physics to date is an E, and she suddenly decides she wanted an A* after the Christmas break, we say that is unrealistic! As far as I am concerned it is not achieving A* that is the impossible task, it is the content that needs to be covered in 4 weeks that makes the goal unrealistic.

Lastly, her goal must have a time limit set by which it would have been achieved. If no time is set, the drive to achieve this will be lacking, moreover, the pitfall of procrastination will be easy to fall into. But when you have a time limit set, you work hard to meet it.

Another example is a goal like this: "I would like to have a healthy and fit body that gives me energy and allows me to enjoy my life."

Based on the SMART formula, this would not be a very good goal statement. It is not specific enough, it's difficult to measure, it contains elements outside your control, and it doesn't have a clear timeline. Smarter goals derived from this statement might look like this:

- I want to lose 34 kg by the end of summer.
- To achieve this I would need to:
- Take 40-minute jogs 3 to 5 times a week
- Eat a reasonable and healthy diet
- Eliminate my habit (take your pick) that negatively impacts my health.
- Keep myself informed, by researching a health related topic once a month. You may even want to break down the goal of eating a reasonable and healthy diet into smarter targets, since it is not very specific or measurable. For instance, you might decide on the following goals:
  - Eat 4 servings of fruit and vegetables every day
  - Limit desserts and pastries to no more than one serving a week
  - Eat half a portion when going out and save the rest for later
  - Limit myself to (at most) one soft-drink per week.

That is a solid goal that was properly thought out and would likely be achieved. Specific and focused!

Let me try and help you here with some of your dreams and goals with the method I learnt and have used since then.

Get a writing pad or an exercise book and a pen:

1. Firstly, write down between 4 to 10 things you have already accomplished and are proud of. Give yourself a pat on the back.
2. What do you want in the next 10 years? This is not what you think you can get, but what you really want, probably something that people have said that you couldn't do. Write down everything that you want.
3. Prioritise the items, give them a tag, like 1 yr goal, or month goal etc.
4. Pick out the 5 most important 1 year goals, and state why they are important to you, (because when the "why" gets stronger, the "how" gets easier.) The object is important, but the purpose must be more powerful than the object.
5. Map out what actions you need to take in order to achieve the goal. What lessons must you take, what research must you do? Who do you need to talk to? Make sure all these are in place.
6. Avoid procrastination: This is very important. It has been said that 'Procrastination is the thief of time,' and we keep postponing, promising ourselves we'll do better. Procrastination eats up a large chunk of our lives, putting things off for another day, so make a start working on your goals now.

Be honest, how many of last year's resolutions did you keep? In this short life we want to accomplish as much as we can, fill our lives with purpose not just for ourselves, but for everyone we come in contact with. We cannot do this if we don't act on our goals. If we don't work on our goals, we won't become the person we would love to become. If we don't become the person we would love to be we will not be happy. If we are not happy in life what else is left?

So the time to take action towards your goals is NOW! You can look back into the past or you can dream of the future, but all you will ever have is right now. The best time to start with your goals in NOW. Do not delay any more.

Chapter 6

THE PRICE AND THE PROMISE

"I hated every minute of training, but I said, 'Don't quit. Suffer now and live the rest of your life as a champion.'"

Mohammed Ali

A few weeks ago, I conducted an assembly for a group of year 7 students (about 240 students). The title of the assembly was "The Price and the Prize". I had spoken about the need to make sacrifices and how easy this can become as soon as we see or understand the reason for them; that it is easier for us to pay the price if we can see the promise.

The reason I thought of that assembly was because, I realise that it is often difficult to inspire kids to do well in school. They just don't see the point of most of the subjects they take.

The most unfortunate thing is that teachers and parents are trying to make their students and their children pay the price without seeing the promise. Sacrificing effort and time is hard enough, but almost unbearable when we cannot see the end result immediately.

The price gets easier and more acceptable if the prize gets larger, or if we can catch a glimpse of it along the way.

My father was financially balanced and my siblings and I lived comfortably as children. When we were young, on our way home my father would sometimes drive us through a very poor neighbourhood. As we enjoyed the ride, he would tell us that the best way to avoid living in these areas was to do well in school. They were not nice areas at all! He also explained to us that hard work was the reason why he could afford to drive good cars and lived in a 5 bedroomed house. He also explained that integrity was the reason he could enjoy what he had with peace of mind! I didn't fully understand why he did what he did or said what he said, but his actions made me want to take care of 3 things:

> I wanted to avoid living in the poor neighbourhood, I wanted to have peace of mind, and I wanted to drive a nice car when I got older. In a very powerful way, it made me more focused on my studies. The *promise* for me was that of not having to live in a ramshackle house and being able to drive a good car. I knew I had to get it right and that the skills and knowledge needed to achieve this were attainable at school.

Suffer now and live the rest
of you life a champion.

Studying very hard to be successful is not easy at all, especially when you were brought up playing with X box. It is hard. But what a small price to pay when we consider the promise of a better tomorrow! An ideal situation would be one in which our parents help us see the promise and encourage us to pay the price. However, we do not always have the ideal situation.

Therefore, it is our responsibility as students to try and understand by asking, what the purpose in sacrificing so much is. Once you see and understand, you will probably be more willing to pay the price. Some time ago a speaker shared his experience of wanting to give up going for his Karate lessons. He was fed up and couldn't cope. His Karate instructor then said "you cannot believe the feeling you get when you can walk up the street alone with no feeling of fear at all." At that moment the speaker changed his mind. "When do I start the class?" He asked. He had seen the promise and was now ready to pay the price.

Now, some people have the benefit of having someone like a father or a role model who provides guidance and the necessary motivation. However, there are many who do not have this opportunity. The truth is that the most important thing is to depend less and less on people to stir you up to do what is right. Self-motivation is priceless, don't always wait for people to come and inspire you before you do the right thing. They may not show up!

The bottom line is that it's not easy to pay the price when we cannot see the promise. If you have the right assurance, then you would do whatever it takes to achieve your dreams. If parents or teachers try to make you pay the price before you clearly see the promise, you are more likely to resist. What can you do for an extraordinary promise? You would sometimes do the most unbelievable things. You can pay if you can see where you are going. Would you engage more in your studies, would you work hard on the project or on that life changing exercise?

As life accumulates, we gather the outcomes or the regrets of our actions. Jim Rohn once said that 'discipline weighs ounces and regrets weigh tonnes'. That therefore suggests that the sacrifices in the long run are nothing compared to the regrets that we feel when we choose to do the wrong things. Sacrifices are indeed a small price to pay!

2 types of Pain:

In life there are always going to be two types of pain. We must experience one or the other. The first type is the pain of sacrifice. No one can deny the fact that spending an extra hour or two away from the game machine, friends or even the TV is not sacrifice for a 12, 13, 15 or 17 year old. It is a lot of sacrifice and it is sort of "painful" for them. Every successful man or woman I know or have read about went through this and you must also go through this type of pain if you are going to make it in life.

For you, the sacrifice may be the hours you spend revising for your biology exams, practising that maths theory or writing that proposal. Sometimes it is the time spent taking extra lessons from Mr Hudson. For one past student of mine, the price she had to pay was going to "Maths help" sessions. She consistently attended these sessions for 3 years, because she realised that Maths was not her strongest subject. She hardly missed any lessons while all her friends were busy playing or doing other 'interesting' stuff. That was the 'pain' she had to suffer. That way she could avoid the pain of regret. How we rejoiced with her as she ended up with a wonderful result and won the award of "personalisation!" for her consistent efforts, focus and achievement.

I read somewhere that Michael Jackson sometimes used to spend 14 hours a day practising his dance moves, and employed the best to take him through the rigours of that exercise. Little wonder he was one of the greatest entertainers in the world! For Ussain Bolt, the pain of sacrifice was the hours of training and perseverance, so he could be the best. Was the sacrifice worth it? You bet it was. Now with millions of pounds worth of contracts and endorsements, it was worth it!

The other type of pain is the pain of regret. These weigh more than the pain of sacrifice. There is nothing as horrible as sitting down and thinking, "Oh I could easily have passed those exams. I knew I could have done better if only I tried harder". It is not a good place to be at all. Some of our actions could cost us our lives or guarantee us a room in prison, and yet it could have been avoided. If, for instance, your friend suggests to you to take part in a riot, the pain of saying "No" and losing that friend is so much lighter than the pain of regret you feel, if you somehow end up injured or in prison!

A student of mine once asked me if it was possible to suffer the 2 types of pain at the same time. That is, someone who put in the effort and didn't make it. My answer to him was, if you have done all you could do, then there is nothing to regret! If you actually put in your best, you leave with the satisfaction that you gave it your best shot and couldn't have done any more. Whatever knowledge or skills you gained by doing your best are always going to be an asset for you in the future! A. L William, once wrote a book titled '*All you can do is all you can do, and all you can do is enough.*' If any boy or girl or even an adult put in his or her very best, that is all anyone can ask of you.

Unfortunately, humans are about the only organism that put in less than their very best in what they do! A tree will grow to its potential and even struggle through diseases to grow to its genetic potential. It will grow as tall as it can grow and the roots will go as deep as they can go to find water, often breaking through rocks. But because human beings have the dignity of choice, we often chose to be less than we can be and achieve much less than our potential! One of the aims of this book is to get you out of this group of people who will do less than they can! Walk away from these people!

I cannot emphasise enough and I will reiterate this time in the words of one of my mentors, Jim Rohn "Walk away from the 97%, don't use their vocabulary, don't use their excuses, and don't use their method of drift and neglect. Let others lead small lives, but not you. Let others argue over small things, but not you. Let others cry over small hurts, but not you. Let others leave their future in someone else's hands, but not you. Walk away! Don't have days like they do, otherwise you will end up broke and poor. Pennies but no treasures and trinkets but no values."

In 1999, Mohammed Ali (formerly Cassius Clay) was voted BBC's Sporting Personality of the Century. What an achievement! To be considered as the best sporting personality in 100 years and to win was an achievement of a lifetime. Many years ago Mohammed Ali made a very important statement, "I hated every minute of training, but I said, 'Don't quit. Suffer now and live the rest of your life as a champion.'"

He refused to live as society has taught us to live, using the "BUY NOW and PAY LATER" philosophy. That means enjoy the benefit of our goods and services and then pay later with your sweat and sometimes blood! It is almost as if the voice keeps telling you to ignore your revision now, avoid the lesson now, ignore that voice of reason now, and do what feels good to you. But what happens later in life? If you end up in a job that you hate, then do not blame life, for life usually rewards hard work. Employers may not always reward hard work, but life often rewards it.

Mohammed Ali suffered then and he is living the rest of his life as a champion. Today he is 70, still referred to as the "champ "and respected all over the world. The state of Kentucky built a centre in his honour. He doesn't have to work anymore as the endorsements provide him with an income for life. He suffered then and now he is a champion for life.

Now, when the project becomes difficult, or when that Maths class or Science class becomes boring to your brain, say to yourself, "suffer now and live my life as a champion!"

When you find yourself saying:

- I hate every minute of my Maths lesson
- I hate every minute of my History lesson
- I hate every minute of my French lesson
- I hate every minute of that exercise programme

Always remember to say to yourself, "Don't quit, I will suffer now and live the rest of my life as a winner!"

Chapter 7

RELATIONSHIPS AND RELATIONAL DISEASES

"It's easy to let influence shape our lives, to let associations determine our direction, to let pressures overwhelm us, and to let tides take us. The big question is, are we letting ourselves become what we wish to become"

Jim Rohn

Most children are greatly influenced by their parents and look to them for support and advice. As they get older and begin to find their place in the world , many youths tend to rely less on their parents and seek advice from their peers. This may be because they feel unable to communicate with their parents or perhaps they need to talk to someone who is closer to their own age. Whatever the reason, it is true to say that your peers can exert a great influence on you.

This influence can be a good thing if your friends are mature and reliable. Sadly, in many cases this influence is not good. Sometimes young people find themselves pressurised into doing things that they know are wrong. Their desire to be accepted by others can lead them to compromise their own beliefs and standards. Some may feel they are strong enough to resist such pressure, but is this a realistic attitude?

Some may find it difficult to accept that, in certain circumstances, peer pressure can be classed as bullying. However, if someone feels pressurised into doing something or acting in a certain way because of fear of rejection or ridicule, then it might be a form of bullying. You should avoid being bullied into doing things you don't want to do.

It is amazing how many lives have been destroyed by the associations they keep. Note that when we talk about peer pressure we are quick to associate it with teenagers and young adults. However, the amount of pressure that unnecessary societal expectations exert on us as people is amazing. It doesn't matter how old you are, where you live, what your background is or what work you do. No one is fully shielded from the effects of peer pressure, until we learn how to say NO to the things we don't really NEED and things that do not contribute to real progress and true happiness.

People have gone into debt because they want "to keep up with the Joneses." They want to drive the same type of car that their neighbours drive or live in the same type of house as their siblings or friends live in.

You, as a teenager, are more exposed to these influences.

Most children spend an unbelievable amount of time watching TV. It is therefore almost as if you are "raised" by the television and the computer. So much time is spent watching TV and it is almost like you know the characters and are therefore easily affected by them. Little wonder then that you can easily be negatively influenced by TV, celebrity lifestyles and other unwholesome role models. You dress like the celebrities you see on TV and think that you can live the type of lives they live.

Peer pressure is an especially powerful force because it is so **subtle**. You do not even realise you are being influenced. It is like a contagious disease or like chloroform. The closer you get to the person or the group, the more you are deprived of the possibility of resisting; the higher your chances of contracting that disease. If you're around smokers, chances are good that you'll be a smoker soon enough. If you are around people who do not study, or people who do not have any good plans for their lives and for their future, chances are excellent that you will be the same.

It is important that we do not underestimate the power of influence. You must realise that positively or negatively, the people you surround yourself with have their attitudes rubbing off on you. If you are around people who are judgemental, spread negative gossip, blame every other person for their problems in life and play victim roles, the chance is greater that you will act the same way too.

To achieve success, you need to start the sorting out process. You need to start getting all the toxic people out of your life; all the energy drainers and dream killers. They don't share your dreams and your passion in life. My father used to say that misery is always looking for company. You don't have to provide company for them anymore. You need to state your dreams and aspirations and give them the chance to change and be an asset in your life or you be an asset in their lives.

They may appreciate you setting new boundaries in your friendship, and rise to the challenge, becoming supportive and positive. But if they don't share your dreams, you need to be "selfish" and think about your life and your future. I don't care who they are or what they represented in the past, if they are dragging you down, you need to replace them, with people or associations that nourish you and bring out the best in you.

There are two types of relationships.

1. *Nourishing relationships*: These are the relationships that inspire you. They share your dreams and passion for achieving goals and they are your greatest cheerleaders. They motivate you, encourage you and advise you from a sincere heart, because they have your

best interests in mind. They will signpost you to where you can get help and be a shoulder to cry on should you need one. They are the members of your "supporters club". Les Brown once said you can run faster with hundred of these people who want to make progress and who are "go getters" than with one negative person around your neck. They will hold you down.

Achievers surround themselves with these kinds of successful people! They want to be around others who are making progress in life and making things happen for themselves. They want to know their secrets and strategies for winning. They are not embarrassed to be hanging out with the "geeks" and the "nerds" of this world who are studying for success and making good progress in life.

You, too, need to surround yourself with positive influences! Join the "groups" that other successful people are in, learn what they are learning, act how they act, and talk how they talk. Be students of good ideas and laudable plans. It doesn't matter what background you are from. Show up and transform yourself into an achiever! Greatness is not just for those who have had it easy, who came from supportive homes or had exclusive "ivy league" education. There are so many successful people who rose up from humble backgrounds and very poor conditions and overcame obstacles to achieve their dreams but they did not get there by hanging out with negative people with no plans and ambitions.

2. *Toxic Relationships:* These are the relationships with people who always criticise you, without constructively showing how you could have done it better. All they can do is find fault and exploit your weaknesses. They will only work with you closely as long as you are for what they are for, or you are against what they are against. They are never into you and they will use you to further their own agenda. They will remind you of the mistakes you have made in

the past. In reality, these people are selfishly trying to reduce you to their level, in order for them to feel better about themselves.

All you need in your life is one of these people close to you and you could let them ruin your whole life. They are not good for your spiritual, physical and mental health. They are energy drainers. I know people who have been ruined because they got stuck with other people who weren't good for them. A lot of people put up with a lot of silliness because they don't want to be alone. They think they would feel lonely if they lose that friend. I have no hesitation in telling you that if you associate yourself with losers, you will end up becoming a loser! Simple! Unconsciously, you will pick up their ways and if care is not taken you will pick up their destinies.

Evaluation:

If you were to do a little bit of a check up on your experiences in life, no matter how young you are, if you assess the major influences in your life, the influences that have made you what you are now are the influences from people you associate yourself with! That is, the people and thoughts you choose to allow into your life. Do not overlook the power of influence. Indeed, the influence of those around us is so powerful! Many times we don't even realize we're being strongly affected because influences generally develop over an extended period of time.

To begin to make real progress, you need to ask yourself some important questions about the effect that your associations are having on you. Ask yourself, "Who am I with most of the time?" Identify the people you spend the majority of your time with. Make a mental or even a written list of these people, these close friends of yours and ask yourself the questions: "Who am I turning into because of this friendship? What is improving in my life and what is getting worse? Are my grades better because of this friendship?"

"What are these friendships or closeness doing to me?" What have they got me doing? Who have they got me listening to? What have they got me reading? Where have they got me going? What do they have me thinking? How have they got me talking? How have they got me feeling? What have they got me saying?" You've got to make a serious study of how others are influencing you, both negatively and positively.

How many people on your list are achieving their dreams, are supporting yours, and are taking responsibility for their lives? How many of them are headed for youth detention centres and prison by virtue of their present attitudes?

You're better off spending time alone than with people who hold themselves and consequently you back with a victim mentality. Simply stop spending time with the negative people on your list. Join the clubs that will put you in touch with a positive circle of friends. Set a new standard for yourself and don't become friends with people who fall below that standard.

You have to take responsibility for this area of your life. Look around you at the people you call friends, you act just like them! Does it make you proud or does it make your parents proud? Are you selling yourself short? Or are you on the right track? Keep successful people around you and you will be successful! Be around people who can accomplish their goals and you will accomplish yours! The choice is yours to make.

Here's a final question: "Is that okay?" Maybe everyone you associate with has been a positive, energizing influence. Then again, maybe there are some bad apples in the bunch. All I'm suggesting here is that you take a close and objective look. Everything is worth serious consideration, especially the power of influence. Both will take you somewhere, but only one will take you in the direction you need to go.

Some people unavoidably live with negative influences. For them my advice will be to shield themselves from their environment. Escape with a good book that will refine your thinking pattern and help shape your dream, rather than you being a captive of that environment. You cannot always change your environment, but you can work on yourself by exposing yourself to written and spoken materials that tend towards your dream!

It is easy to just dismiss the things that influence our lives. One man says, "I live here, but I don't think it matters. I'm around these people, but I don't think it hurts." I would take another look at that. Remember, everything matters! Sure, some things matter more than others, but everything amounts to something. You've got to keep checking to find out whether your associations are tipping the scales towards the positive or towards the negative. Ignorance is never the best policy, finding out is!

I have just read the story of the little bird. The bird had his wing over his eye and he was crying. The owl said to the bird, "You are crying."

"Yes," said the little bird, and he pulled his wing away from his eye.

"Oh, I see," said the owl. "You're crying because the big bird pecked out your eye."

And the little bird said, "No, I'm not crying because the big bird pecked out my eye. I'm crying because I let him."

Many years from now, you may be crying, not because your life ended up being poor and useless, but because you allowed it!

Chapter 8

THE WEAPONS OF MASS DISTRACTION

"By prevailing over all obstacles and distractions, one may unfailingly arrive at his chosen goal or destination."-Christopher Columbus

There is no doubt that friends can be a major clog in the wheel of our progress. They can help by influencing us positively, and they can also influence us negatively. As previously discussed, though the effect of friends can be subtle, it is more obvious than some other factors that can affect our lives and make it difficult for us to achieve our goals.

These other factors are what I call the weapons of mass distraction. They are seemingly harmless, extremely useful and mostly fun, but as far as our future is concerned, they can be deadly if not properly used.

Deadly, because they can stop us from achieving our goals and becoming the person we would like to be. This is especially true of teenagers and school children who have little control over their actions.

Before I make my list, I want to emphasize that all the weapons are not negative in themselves, in fact some are very good when you are in control, but they have the ability to hold you down and keep you bound. When this happens, they become weapons of mass distraction and they can distract you from your dreams and negatively affect your destiny.

For a boy or girl on a mission of making it in life, you must make every minute count. Once you have set your mind on success, you will find many weapons of mass distraction that will attempt to rob you of focusing solely on taking care of what matters to you at that time.

E-MAIL:

As we all know, it is a very important means of communication. However, sometimes when we open our emails, we are bombarded with a lot of irrelevant information. Some of these emails do not have any relevance to us and some are from unknown senders. Going through some of those emails takes a lot of our time and will deprive us of valuable time for study or other important things we need to do. Sort through your emails quickly, respond first to emails that have to do with study/work and act on those immediately. Respond to emails from friends who have questions or situations needing your attention. Interact positively and get the best out of the mail. This is not the time to open emails with forwarded jokes or pictures of cute animals dressed up in formal gowns, with the intent of putting a smile on your face. This in itself is great, but can be time wasting and can distract you from your goal. It is better to postpone the reading of such emails until a later time, when you do not have deadlines to meet or when you have finished all the work that needs to be done. I love to "chill out," but there is nothing like chilling out when your mind is free and you don't have deadlines hanging over your head. Emails can sometimes be a DISTRACTION!!!

SKYPE.

Skype and other instant messengers like Yahoo and msn are very vital tools of communication, but they are very addictive and you should avoid the temptation of starting a conversation when you have deadlines to meet, or you have tests coming up. Alternatively, Skype can be used as a revision tool with your friends. In fact, I used to teach a friend's son science using Skype. But, if you don't have control, you can spend the whole day on Skype with little to show for the time spent! In fact I suggest that you discipline yourself and have set times for using these tools. From experience, I know that once you start, you may end up spending valuable time; minutes quickly becoming hours. If a friend has left you messages on Skype, rapidly respond to these, but avoid the temptation to make a Skype return call. We all know it'll turn into a time waster. And, definitely postpone calls of a personal nature until you have finished, as some of these can become time wasters. Reward yourself with this call when you finish that important piece of coursework or assignment. DISTRACTION!

SOCIAL MEDIA.

Using social media such as Twitter or Facebook is extremely effective in expanding your circle of influence and depending on the business you do, it can be a valuable tool in helping one another and sharing useful information, doing homework and helping one another to solve academic problems. The only problem is, it can be a big time waster, if not used properly.

I see some funny status messages and I laugh. "James is having a shower and enjoying vanilla ice-cream!" When I have work to do, it wouldn't matter to me if he had a bath or a shower or if it was chocolate or vanilla ice-cream! It is amazing the number of people who post their problems without doing anything about them! If you have a problem seek for a solution, posting it on Facebook doesn't really help. It rather gives a topic for the next round of gossip in town.

The clock is ticking, there is zero time to read and answer personal messages. Simply open, read and answer any communication that is relevant to your work, studies or that helps in your pursuit of excellence. Leave the rest for later. They are best enjoyed, and you can relax with these when you have finished your study. With Twitter, it is the same. Some of the tweets have valuable information, so I take what is useful and leave the rest. Reading the millions of irrelevant tweets that fill your screen? DISTRACTION, especially when you have work to complete.

PHONE CALLS and SMS (TEXT MESSAGES).

There is perhaps no greater waste of your time than the telephone and its first cousin, the short message service. More so when you get a dear friend, who wants to give you every excruciating detail of her day. Please do not get me wrong, you need to be there for your friends, and give them a listening ear and a shoulder to cry on. But, you need to be conscious of the time while you do this, especially when you have very important things to take care of.

The simplest solution for these interruptions: let your answering machine handle these DISTRACTIONS, not you. I read the story of a man whose elder aunt would call and speak to his answering machine as though it was part of his family. She calls it four or five times in a row to keep adding to her original message. Imagine taking the time to talk to her? That is 4 hours gone out of your day. You cannot afford that.

A friend of mine mentioned how addicted her daughter is to text messages. She said "Students just don't get it! They think it is their right to come into lessons with mobile phones, so they do not miss the 'lifesaving' message that may come in." I think this is true, but you can be the exception to the rule. You cannot be a slave to a piece of equipment. Use it as much as you require, but be in control! Even for some adults they can be addictive. How many lives have been lost as a result of our addiction to this wonderful gadget, often used at the wrong time? I am talking about car accidents as a result of someone driving and texting! Texting affects our concentration while driving, studying or doing other important stuff. It can also affect so many areas of our lives by reducing our ability to focus and thereby robbing us of a good life! DISTRACTION.

TELEVISION.

TV can easily become the biggest time thief of all and yet, people don't realize it. It is amazing how people take the time to buy the best security for their home so their precious belongings don't get stolen, but when it comes to protecting their mind and their time, two of their biggest assets, the doors are wide open for easy pickings.

Try to focus on what is
infront of you.

The X Factor, Grey's Anatomy, Scrubs, Britain's got Talent, etc. Great TV shows. I love watching these shows, although I usually make sure I do all that needs to be done before I can allow myself the luxury of watching them. In a way, they help, because they make us work hard and finish any domestic and school work, knowing full well that we are going to relax and enjoy these shows as a reward. You too need to get your priorities right. If you find yourself watching hours of television every day, it might be good to think about whether or not it's a subtle indication to yourself that your life is not what you want it to be, that it's not interesting enough, so you feel the need to immerse yourself in the lives of others.

I am not suggesting that you live your life as I do, I am only saying there are a lot of distracting factors out there, almost bordering on addictions. This is the worst part of watching too much television. Brian Kim once said that TV can be just as addictive as any illegal substance on the market today. It's easily accessible, pleasurable, and makes you forget your troubles for the day!

"You watch one show and when it ends, the TV says 'Coming up next . . . stay tuned for blah blah blah', so you become curious, you watch it and you like it and BOOM, you add another programme to your weekly TV schedule. Those hours add up and once you get vested in the shows, they've got you for life!"

I cannot help asking myself how much money they pay people, especially when I see the dedication to some of these programmes on TV, like football. Don't get me wrong, I enjoy watching a good game of football and I do play football when I have the opportunity or as part of my fitness regime. But, to ignore my planning time or my study time at the expense of watching these games will make me less productive than I can be. DISTRACTIONS! So what should you do? If you have a game of football to watch, make it part of your plan for the day. Set out what you need to achieve that day and what you need to do in order to relax.

I am looking forward to the Olympic Games, in fact I cannot wait for it to start. So, I am getting all that needs to be done out of the way so I can enjoy the games!

"What Katie Price did next," Oh my God! What have we got ourselves into? I am honestly not interested in what Katie did next, neither do I want to be keeping up with the Kardashians, I am busy trying to build a future for myself and my family. A half-hour of this DISTRACTION will turn into an hour or two or three and there goes your valuable study or preparation time. If you must watch a programme, why don't you record it with the new Sky technology and watch it later when you are done with your work?

These are very basic distractions. I'm sure you can think of and have experienced more. Your objective in building your life, and working hard is to delay pleasure and suffer pain now so you can enjoy your life tomorrow. Like I said earlier, don't be caught up in what the world is selling to us. That is the "BUY NOW and PAY LATER" philosophy. They are basically saying enjoy now and pay with your life later, rather than saying sacrifice now so you can have a good future, where you can talk for 2 hours on the phone if you like and it doesn't affect you in any way!

Be wise and avoid the WEAPONS OF MASS DISTRACTION!

Chapter 9

TIME MANAGEMENT

"Don't be fooled by the calendar. There are only as many days in the year as you make use of. One man gets only a week's value out of a year while another man gets a full year's value out of a week."-Charles Richards

Wikipedia defines time management as the act or process of planning and exercising conscious control over the amount of time spent on specific activities, especially to increase effectiveness, efficiency or productivity. Time is a very precious commodity. There are two major things that make every man equal; death and time. The poorest man and the richest man will both die one day. Also, the richest man and the poorest man both have 24 hours in a day. No rich man has ever been able to buy extra hours for his children. So we are all stuck with only 24 hours in a day. The onus is therefore on us to make the most of the time available.

You can waste your ice-cream, you can be wasteful and throw away clothes. You can waste money and then make more. But wasted time? That is a whole different situation. I am not talking about the 2 hours you want back after watching a bad movie. I'm talking about the time you feel you wasted watching hours on end of TV, while you neglected your English homework and your Maths revision. And for older ones, the time you wasted staying in a relationship with the wrong person for years. It's one of the biggest regrets in life. Not because we know we can't get the time back.

We all know that. But because we torture ourselves with "What could've been." What you could've done with that time and as a result, where you would be today.

Now what do we take from all this? A resolve not to waste time again. But we find we inevitably do it again. The truth is—**you'll NEVER know where you might be now had you not "wasted your time".** So don't waste any more time wondering about it. It is a further waste of time!

So what can we do to avoid the regrets associated with time or how can you manage your time better? I will share a few tips that I have used successfully to manage my time better and achieve so much more. You can always adjust these to fit into your own specific lifestyle.

1. Have a "to do list"

I while ago, I realised that any time I start my day without a "to do list", I always ended up doing less and wasting so much time on minor things. I always wondered how fast time went and why I was not able to achieve as much. Nothing can be as horrible as to be busy doing nothing! That is what normally happens when you start your day without a plan. You need to make your to do list specific so that you don't miss the major tasks or overlook something important.

2. Avoid taking on too much

One of the things that can take away valuable time from you is your inability to say "No" to people. If so, you will probably have far too many items or commitments on your list. This will eventually lead to poor performance and inadequate management of your time. If you have too many tasks on your list, you may end up being the "guy" that produces rushed and sloppy work. To stop this, learn the subtle art of saying "yes" to the person, but "no" to the task. This skill helps you assert yourself, while still maintaining good feelings within the group.

3. Avoid Procrastination

It is also very important that we avoid procrastination. If you have a task to do, just go ahead and do it. The time will never be perfect, so do not put off what you need to do. Our parents promised to do so many things later, but never got round to it. "I will get started when the kids are out of school" they said.' "I'll do it when the kids go back to school." They never did. Time keeps moving, even if you do not. If you have the ability to begin work on a task or even your goals today, don't wait until tomorrow.

I have decided to stop procrastinating and get my Science work done... I will start tomorrow!

4. Avoid distractions

There are a lot of unnecessary distractions that we face every day in our modern world. Many of you lose as much as 4 hours a day to distractions. Think how much you could get done if you had that time back! They may come from emails, IM chats, colleagues, or even a phone call or text from your mum. Such phone calls or texts could have waited. If you want to gain control of your day and do your best work, it's vital to know how to reduce these distractions and manage interruptions effectively. For instance, turn off your IM chat when you need to focus, and let people know if they're distracting you too often.

5. Take Regular Breaks

It would be lovely if we can work without any stopping, especially when we have a deadline to meet, but it is not realistic and definitely not healthy to just keep going without breaks. It's impossible for anyone to focus and produce really high-quality work without giving their brains some time to rest and recharge. So, don't dismiss breaks as "wasting time." They provide valuable down-time, which will enable you to think creatively and work effectively. Schedule breaks for yourself, or set an alarm as a reminder. Go for a quick walk, chat to friends or just do something that takes your mind off your work. Try to take a 5, 10, 20 or 30 minute break or more depending on what task you have or how many hours you have available. You won't produce top quality work if you're hungry or too tired!

These are just a few tips about managing your time. Be wise and treat time with respect!

Chapter 10

LEADERSHIP!

*"A good objective of leadership is to help those who are doing poorly
to do well and to help those who are doing well to do even better."*

—*Jim Rohn*

I have learnt a lot about leadership in my life and especially this past decade, from my father and Mr Rohn. I am so happy to share their tried and tested wisdom and tips about leadership. First of all you need to realise that the journey of a carefully planned life will not just end in success. It will also be a journey into leadership. There is no other way to build massive long-term success than to deserve it. The level of success you have will be directly proportional to the values you put in other people's lives.

To have the opportunity to put values into another person's life, you must become a leader. You do not have to become a named leader, like director of this or coordinator of that, but true success leads you into a place or position of some kind of leadership or the other. When this happens, you must be ready to provide strong directional leadership, hence the need to learn the skills necessary to provide this.

Leadership is the ability to inspire yourself, in such a way that you become worthy of inspiring and leading others. It can sometimes be expressed as the power to influence and persuade someone to adopt a way of life or buy/

sell a product. Alternatively, it could be that they have a good idea, and you are working in their favour and on their side.

We all have the chance to provide leadership and influence. Often times we are already providing a form of leadership, and the earlier we understand that and lead properly, the better it is going to be for us and for those we provide leadership to.

For instance, some of the people we know could be recognised leaders depending on what we do. An example could be a head teacher of a school. You don't have to be the head teacher to provide leadership, as a teacher you are the leader in your classroom. As a parent, you are leading a household, or as the first child you are providing leadership to your siblings. People look up to you even without realising that they are. They see and follow what you do more than simply doing what you tell them!

Jim Rohn made a profound statement some time ago which summarises what leadership should be about, and I personally have learnt a lot from him and freely share his insights. He said "Leaders go from communicating to connecting! Speak, listen, observe and write. Master those skills. Speaking is not merely talking, Listening is not merely hearing, observing is not merely seeing and writing is not merely scribbling."

"What other leadership experience do you have apart from... beating up your brother, feeding the cats and walking the dog?"

If you are a class captain or the "head boy", you must be connecting with your colleagues. Remember how you got to this place and do not ignore the need of the people and the need to connect with them. The best way to connect will be firstly to identify with the people you are leading. Let them know, not just by talking, but by doing, that you truly care for their welfare. Have a remarkable idea that you will share, and open a dialogue with them. Make your point with tact. Tact has been described as the ability to make a point without making an enemy.

You must become a student of good ideas and you must be a good observer. Never allow a day to pass without attempting to find answers to important questions; questions that have the potential to affect your team; questions about current events in your company, or in your group. What are the new breakthroughs, the new opportunities, the tools and techniques that are current? Who are the new people influencing your world, and the local opinion? You must become skilful evaluators of all that is going on around us. All events affect you, and what affects us leaves a mark on who we will be one day and how we will one day live.

Often, the most extraordinary opportunities are hidden among the seemingly insignificant events of life. If we do not pay attention to these events, we can easily miss the opportunities, and perhaps more importantly; fail the people we lead. The more we are aware of these, the more we are able to nourish them like a mother would, and protect like a father. You must be like a father and a mother to those you provide leadership to. You see something in them before they could see it in themselves, and bring them out of discouragement and into positivity. Be ready to give your time and your attention. You cannot be selfish and be a leader!

John Kennedy once said, "Don't ask what the country (government, parents, etc.) can do for you, but ask what I can do for the country (my parents, my school, my community)." What can I do for my teacher, my mother, my father, my son? You don't become successful or have high self-esteem or recognition by asking what your friend can do for you, but by asking yourself what you can do for them.

As a leader, it is important to get people to work together. You should never be a divisive force. Getting people to work together is magic. It is very challenging, but once you figure out how, it's exciting. The best approach for a leader, be it a teenager or a head of department, is to use the "let's go do it" approach. Not "you go do it," but LET'S GO DO IT!

Reward your members. It could be a handshake, pat on the back or a card, just to show that you care and you appreciate them. Reward your younger brother or sister and you may forever change the dynamism of your relationship for the better.

Inspire by your testimonies. "If I can do it, you can do it, if Jane can do it you can do it." Help them see themselves better than they are. My father was very good at this. He saw so much in us before we could see it. He encouraged us, and was a great cheerleader. No one believed in us as he did. And so should you. Help them to see themselves as they are. If they make mistakes, tell them they must be corrected. Tell them they have missed it, but don't leave them in the mess. Help them to see themselves better than they are; to see what they can be in the future.

Learn to work with people who deserve you, not those who need you. Be like life itself. Life responds to people who deserve it, not just people who need its help. Help people to deserve your help and attention.

Become A Good Listener

This is very difficult in our world today, because of the various voices that continually want our attention. It is therefore our responsibility to try and be careful with the things we listen to.

Whenever we hear these voices, which may be from those we are providing leadership for, we must stop and assess the messages. We must not ignore without first considering. But if after consideration the message is without substance or if it is not moving towards the realisation of our goal, we must tactfully move on! However, when you hear a message that is valuable, then you have to take time to process it and see how it might benefit you and your group.

We become better communicators when we have learnt to be good listeners. Listening is said to be an opportunity to add to our knowledge and to increase our value.

Be well informed.

A leader must be sound in knowledge. Learn as you go along and realise that many people will look up to you. Read as many good books as possible. Men and women of experience have offered their experiences in written and spoken form so that we can be inspired and instructed by them, and so that we can amend our thinking patterns by their ideas. Their contributions enable us to re-plan our lives based on their experiences and avoid their errors.

"Reading is essential for those who seek to rise above the ordinary. We must not permit anything to stand between us and the book that could change our lives. A little reading each day will result in a wealth of valuable information in a very short period of time. But if we fail to set aside the time, if we fail to pick up the book, if we fail to exercise the discipline, then ignorance will quickly move in to fill the space." J Rohn

Lastly, it is also important to study leadership patterns and I believe there is nothing wrong with learning from great leaders. There are many leadership styles and strategies for you to choose from. It's your decision about how you want to lead, but you *MUST lead*.

"Atilla the Hun" was a leader hundreds of years ago, but, he was hated by his men and was stabbed in the back by his wife. He led by fear and intrigue. Mobutu Seseseko was a leader. He led by fear and terrorized his men. Jesus was (is) a leader. His followers loved him and they continued his teachings for thousands of years. He led by example and he led through love.

I believe a great leader must be a servant leader; one who leads by example and serves the people. Service first to those who deserve it, and then to those who need it. Yes, leadership is all about service. There are, however, certain qualities that must be found in the servant leader. You may want to find out if you have some of these qualities, and see where you need to make amends.

1. Visions: Can you see the big picture for you and your team?
2. Purpose: Do you have enough reasons to keep going when people say "no?"
3. Rapport: Are you respectful and responsive to your team members and colleagues?
4. Action: Will you do what you must do?
5. Service: Do you help those who deserve your help?
6. Belief: How certain are you of the validity of your mission or of the project at hand?

7. Excellence: Will you settle for less than the best or constantly demand improvement?
8. Persistence: Will you quit before you get to your destination?
9. Teamwork: Do you recognise the synergy of people working together?
10. Communication: Are you mastering the skills of listening and communicating?
11. Commitment: Are you really committed to your team and to your organisation?
12. Confidence: Are you really certain you will make it?
13. Health: Do you take care of your body, soul and spirit?
14. Love: Will you remember that in the end, love is all that really matters?
15. Sincerity: Will you lead through integrity or will you follow in the way of the multitude?

These questions beg for answers. To be a true leader you must be a servant leader with these qualities and more.

Lastly, I will be remiss if I failed to share with you the necessity of the leader not to send feelers of defeat to their team mates. I learnt that lesson from a dear friend in France a few years ago when I was leading a team of over 1,000 in a multinational network marketing company.

You see, it has been said that "if you are up, go down, and if you are down, go up". One beautiful thing about life is even as leaders, we also have leaders and those we respect in our chosen field. They are supposed to know (at least theoretically) more than we do. It is to them that we turn to when we have a feeling of concern, anxiety or depression.

We should for no reason negatively impact the people we lead by taking our negativity down the line. Therefore, it is when we are "up" emotionally that it is the best time to talk with those you provide leadership to. Do not, and I repeat DO NOT share your depression and tears with anyone junior to you in the team you lead. You could poison a huge percentage of your organisation by doing so. It can be very discouraging for a new member to discover that his or her leader is uncertain about a situation, or that they are down emotionally about a course of action. Avoid sharing angry complaints and depression with your team. The fact that their team leader is depressed will cause them to question the workability of the project or task, and start to doubt themselves.

Ere closing this chapter I would like to share these sublime words on this same issue from the ready pen of Phil Stenberg, a friend of mine in France:

"Whether in teaching or traditional business, complaining to your staff is like sawing off the branch you are sitting on. Raising complaints against your subordinates is like setting your own home on fire with your family locked inside. Your own leaders are for that! Scream, bite, hit, threaten but always to those above you."

"Remember that it is the main quality of a leader to look good, as if all is well. Can you imagine the boss of a company, coming half crying to work and saying, 'we are almost bankrupt' or 'we have the worst manufacturing manager.' Would the staff stay? Not even for that day. Then for sure, 100%, that company is dead!"

Chapter 11

PHILOSOPHY OF THE ANTS

"Go to the ant, thou sluggard; consider her ways, and be wise"

Proverb 6:6

There is a piece of advice found in proverb. It advises us to "go to the ant" and "consider her ways, and be wise". I have thought about the advice and concluded that there must be something worthwhile to learn from the ant for that advice to have been given. Over the last summer holiday, I put on my scientist cap and went to my back garden. Not only did I physically observe the ants, I also did a lot of research into what other notable scientists have done. What I already knew and what I studied was interesting. I will therefore share with you the facts and wisdom of the ANTS.

There are over 10,000 known species of ants. Some ants sleep seven hours a day! Ants can lift 20 times their own body weight. The abdomen of the ant contains two stomachs. One stomach holds the food for itself and the second stomach is for food to be shared with other ants! Each colony of ants has its own smell. In this way, intruders can be recognized immediately.

Ants are self-motivated

The first evident fact I learnt about the ant is the fact that they are self-motivated. I watched an ant trying to move a dead insect over 5 times its body size. He didn't need to wait for any other ants to come and encourage him before trying. What also amazed me was the persistence. He kept trying and would move round and round to see if there was an easier way. But he kept at it. You must be self-motivated to do what is right and good for you.

Ants are hard-working:

Another trait that can easily be seen by watching ants is their hard work. They seem to be working all the time. Therein lies the secret to their success. They adopt the "do all you can" attitude.

How much will an ant gather during summer to prepare for the winter? All he possibly can. We can adopt the same "do all you can" attitude. Give more than what is expected. Why give 50% when you can give 110%? The difference between a victim and a victor is often their mentality. Victims try to shrink from their responsibilities. To achieve anything in life, we must be hard working. Hard work never kills anyone, but laziness will rob you of a bright future. Learn from the ants!

Ants are very focused:

Ants are extremely focused in their ways. I remember the ant I saw trying to move a dead insect. It continued and tried until it started moving it gradually. I was watching to see if it would look around for smaller insects, which were all around it, but it started with this and it continued. If there had been a mobile phone in the world of the ant, I am sure they would have hidden it somewhere so they could focus on the task at hand. Sooner or later, the ant would make it and succeed at moving the insect, just because it is focused on this one task. Single minded indeed.

Ants are great team players and are extremely organized

Ants are social insects, living in organised colonies, that is, a group of cooperating individuals. They may be organised in various ways. A typical ant colony contains a single fertile queen and numerous sterile workers. Communication is coordinated largely by secretions called pheromones. Ants are clean and tidy insects. Some worker ants are given the job of taking the rubbish from the nest and putting it outside in a special rubbish dump. Ants are very great team players, very cooperative, with each having its specific work and faithfully carrying out their duties and obligations to the colony. One will see an item of interest to them and may try to carry it. Before long, there are 70 ants helping out in that task. This is why ants are such successful animals. I once watched a documentary showing ants crossing a bridge with their queen. It is such a beauty to behold. The cooperation, shared determination and skills! What a way to live! We must be organised in our thoughts, we must organise our plans and we must be organised in the things we do.

Ants run away fast when something harmful is around

Ants don't play "superman" unnecessarily. So many people see danger and go in that direction. The ants avoid danger. So should you. Run as fast as possible from friends and foes who would hurt you or situations that can harm you. Be as wise as the ant.

Ants help and share with others

The abdomen of the ant contains two stomachs. One stomach holds the food for itself and the second stomach is for food to be shared with other ants. What a way to live! Life should never be for "me, myself and I". We must learn to share what we have with our fellow humans and help them in their times of need. If a worker ant finds a good source of food, it leaves a trail of scent so that the other ants in the colony can find it. Now, that is an impressive thing to do. The ability to point others to the food supply and source of sustenance is commendable. That, my friend, is how to live the good life.

Ants understand timing

Ants think summer all winter.

During winter, ants remind themselves, "this won't last long—we'll soon be out of here," and on the first warm day, the ants are out. If it turns cold again, they'll dive back down, but then they come out on the next warm day. They can't wait to get out and start working and making progress. From time to time, we may hit rock bottom. Sometimes, it seems like the whole of the world is against us. Always remind yourself to stay positive despite your circumstances, do not lose hope or be discouraged. We all experience failure, disappointment, rejection and setbacks. Yes it hurts, and that is ok. But it won't last forever. Be like the ant.

Ants never quit.

Try to stop them from getting to somewhere they are heading for, study how they find ways to look for another way to get to their destination. They'll climb around, they'll climb under, and they'll climb over. They keep looking for alternatives. Truly fantastic! They never quit looking for a way to get to where they want to go. You too should be like that!

Ants are good financial managers

I often wonder why many people cannot just act like little ants, that seem to understand the importance of saving. Recently I have started imitating our little friends to improve my *financial security*. Ants always save in times of plenty, in order to survive when things get tough. As much as I can, I see to it that I have at least a few savings in my bank account. Before that, I always had reasons why I couldn't save every month, but I am done with giving excuses and have started to act on what I learnt from the ants. I wish I started that earlier in my life, but it is better late than never!

Now, you have the wisdom of the ants. Your parents give you money to spend in school. Please don't spend everything on food and sweets! Even if it is a pound a day, it will be useful to you one day. Don't just consume all you have as if there is no tomorrow. Learn from the ants!

There is an old fable about the grasshopper and the ant that I once read and in ending this chapter, I would like to share the story with you.

In a field one summer's day a grasshopper was hopping about, chirping and singing to its heart's content. A group of ants walked by, grunting as they struggled to carry plump kernels of corn. "Where are you going with those heavy things?" asked the grasshopper. Without stopping, the first ant replied, "To our ant hill. This is the third kernel I've delivered today."

"Why not come and sing with me," teased the grasshopper, "instead of working so hard?"

"We are helping to store food for the winter," said the ant, "and think you should do the same."

"Winter is far away and it is a glorious day to play," sang the grasshopper.

The ants went on their way and continued their hard work. The weather soon turned cold. All the food lying in the field was covered with a thick white blanket of snow that even the grasshopper could not dig through. Soon the grasshopper found itself dying of hunger.

He staggered to the ants' hill and saw them handing out corn from the stores they had collected in the summer. He begged them for something to eat.

"What!" cried the ants in surprise, "haven't you stored anything away for the winter? What in the world were you doing all last summer?"

"I didn't have time to store any food," complained the grasshopper; "I was so busy playing music that before I knew it the summer was gone."

The ants shook their heads in disgust, turned their backs on the grasshopper and went on with their work.

May you never end up like the grasshopper!

Chapter 12

Never Give up!

"It's not that I'm so smart, it's just that I stay with problems longer."

—*Albert Einstein*

I have never ceased to be amazed by the number of people who quit in life or give up on their dreams. I didn't understand why people could quit on dreams that are sometimes so laudable and achievable and that could be so beautiful and so rewarding, until I later realised that quitting is something that we see in every industry. People from different parts of the world quit. Insurance agents will tell you the same story. Bankers quit, programmers quit. In fact, someone once told me of an IBM interview where 50% of the people who qualified for the interview didn't show up. They quit before they started! The temptation is not just for you. *But you can make a difference.* You must be committed to your dreams. Most people never make it because they quit too early.

FAILURE CANNOT HANDLE PERSISTENCE. Persistence always wins in the end!" Calvin Coolidge once wrote: *"Nothing in the world can take the place of persistence. Talent will not. Nothing is more common than unsuccessful men with talent. Genius will not. Unrewarded genius is almost a proverb. Education will not. The world is full of educated derelict. Persistence and determination alone are omnipotent."*

If there is one big thing I would like you to learn from this book, it is that you *must* not give up on your dreams. Don't stop dreaming because you failed the first, second or the third time. Don't stop dreaming because someone else does not believe in your dreams or because your attempts didn't succeed at once.

Thomas Edison tried about 10,000 experiments before he created the first successful light bulb. He didn't give up, and became one of the most prolific inventors of all time with over 1,000 patents to his name. He later said about his failed attempts at the electric lamp; "I have not failed. I have just found 10,000 ways that didn't work!" what an idea! He also said that "many of life's failures are people who did not realize how close they were to success when they gave up." He didn't give up, and he became a great advocate for hard work. "Genius" he said, "is one per cent inspiration, ninety-nine per cent perspiration"

J.K Rowling, the author, whose book *Harry Potter,* was rejected by 12 publishers over a long period of time before one accepted her work. Now she is richer than the queen of England because she didn't give up. She said, (and I love this quote) "You might never fail on the scale I did. But it is impossible to live without failing at something, unless you live so cautiously that you might as well not have lived at all in which case, you fail by default." What a philosophy. What was her message? "Please don't give up!"

John Grisham, one of my favourite authors, was first a lawyer who started writing after he witnessed a case. The book, A *Time to Kill* took three years to write. The book was rejected by 28 publishers before Wynwood Press, an unknown publisher, agreed to give it a modest 5,000-copy printing. He could have given up the 27th time and would have been a loser. He has sold over 250 million copies of his books as of 2008 and was the worldwide top-selling author of the 90s.

Albert Einstein is today known as the face of modern Physics. He didn't talk until he was 4 and couldn't read until he was 7. He was awarded the 1921 Nobel Prize for Physics for his explanation of the photoelectric effect in 1905 and "for his services to Theoretical Physics". However, when Einstein was young, his parents thought he was mentally retarded. His grades in school were so poor that a teacher asked him to quit, saying, **"Einstein, you will never amount to anything!"** Einstein didn't give up on his own abilities. He persisted and the rest is now history!

Winston Churchill failed sixth grade. He failed his examination to the Royal Military College twice. He didn't give up. He tried again and it was at the third attempt that he managed to pass the entrance examination. Once there, he applied himself seriously to school work. With a speech impediment, he didn't have much chance as a politician. He was subsequently defeated in every election for public office until he became Prime Minister at the age of 62. He later wrote, "Never give in, never give in, never, never, never, never—in nothing, great or small, large or petty—never give in except to convictions of honour and good sense. Never, Never, Never, Never give up!

Colonel Sanders, the founder of KFC, started his dream at 65 years old! (This should inspire the older readers. You are never too old to achieve your dreams. My father was 86 years old when he died; he was writing the 6th chapter of his 4th book. He was not slowed down by age!) Colonel Sanders suspected that owners of cafes would love his fried chicken recipe, use it, and sales would increase; and he would get a percentage. He drove around the country knocking on doors, sleeping in his car, wearing his white suit. Do you know how many times people said no until he got one yes? **1009 times! Never give up!**

Michael Jordan is arguably one of the greatest basketball players of all time. He was a great athlete with a unique combination of grace, power, speed and great skills. However, this same Jordan was rejected from his high school basketball team because of his "lack of skills". He refused to let failure stop him. He was once quoted as saying, "I have missed more than 9,000 shots in my career. I have lost almost 300 games. On 26 occasions I have been entrusted to take the game winning shot, and I missed. I have failed over and over and over again in my life. And that is why I succeed!"

There are countless examples of famous people who made it after years of not giving up. They are setting good examples for us, never to give up! But you see, man's first instinct under pressure is to run, to extricate or remove himself from the situation. When we run from a problem or give up, we immediately flunk the test. If we must be winners in life we cannot be sluggards or quitters. Nothing can defeat us except our own *unbelief.*

Many years ago my father gave me a book titled "100 Great Lives". I read of a young man who was not given any chance to make it big in life. He had no beauty or charming smile to pave the way for him. In fact, his own father's description of him was. *"He looked as if he had been badly cut with an axe and needed smoothing with a jackplane."*

His goal was to become a member of the legislature. Now, that is a high goal for a man to try to reach, especially when starting small in life. He joined politics, strove manfully, and was defeated. So he decided he should go into business. The result was that he went bankrupt and spent many years paying off the bad debt of his crooked partner who drank and used up the entire sales stock , while the young man was busy with his face buried in his books. He started a law practice and it was a failure. He fell in love with a beautiful woman and death snatched her out of his hand. Then he decided to be a full time politician. He ran for congress and lost. Twice he became a candidate for the senate and was defeated. He became a candidate for the vice-presidency, and he was rejected.

If any had reason to quit, this man did! He had a young son who was the darling of his life. And the boy died. Did he give up? No, he didn't, though many a lesser man would have. Today, in Washington D. C. you can look up into his face filled with sorrow and compassion and yet with a certain determination as he sits there in his great white chair in the Lincoln monument and looks down upon the union he saved and the slaves he freed. He didn't quit! He became an over comer. He prevailed and made it to the *throne* (of the United States of America). Abraham Lincoln, though dead, still speaks to me and to you!

Ah! My young friend, you may feel you have failed in every opportunity you have been given in life so far. Or that you have messed up every chance of achieving success in your school work. I've got news for you! The race is still on. You can still make a difference; you can start correcting the errors of the past, so that you can make something out of your life. It is better late than never. We are not made for defeat.

Are you at a crossroad, in your life? Do you feel overwhelmed with problems at school or at home? Do you feel like you are a failure? Do you feel like giving up on that dream? You are closer to victory than you imagine. Strength, my friend, springs out of weakness! Life emerges out of death! Victory is secured in the heat of battle! The 'crown' of success goes only to those who stick it to the end. Quitters receive no crowns, the fearful go empty handed, but he who endures till the end shall be successful!

About the Author

Tola Adeliyi is a Teacher of Science, Youth Impact Coach and a Motivational Speaker. He is a graduate of Animal Biology from the University of Agriculture, Abeokuta, Nigeria and got his Postgraduate Certificate in Education from the prestigious University of Warwick, England. Before his teaching career, He was at different times, the Managing Partner of Archon Ventures Ltd and Golden Domains Ltd based in Lagos. He was also the team leader of one of the largest teams (2,000) representing ForMor International, an American company based in Conway, Arkansas.

Photography by Collin Bright

He is widely travelled and was involved in organising and giving lectures regularly on *Motivation, Nutrition* and *Healthy Living* to audiences of between 50 and 800 in more than 30 countries, in 3 continents. He holds motivational talks to encourage youth/older groups to be purposeful and achieve their full potential in life. He is a member of the National Association of Speakers Clubs, UK.

Currently, he is the SEN coordinator and Director of the Excellence Department at the Hazeley Academy, Milton Keynes, UK. He lives in Milton Keynes with his family.

For more information or speaking engagement e-mail
info@impactforsuccess.co.uk or visit *www.impactforsuccess.co.uk*

Recommended Reading

Five Major Pieces of the Life Puzzle by Jim Rohn

The Art of Exceptional Living by Jim Rohn

You were Born Rich by Bob Procter

The Richest Man in Babylon by George Clason

It's Not Over Until You Win by Les Brown

All You Can Do Is All You Can Do And All You Can Do Is Enough by Art Williams

Live Your Dreams by Les Brown

Dream Can Still Come True With Network Marketing by Tola Adeliyi

Printed in Poland
by Amazon Fulfillment
Poland Sp. z o.o., Wrocław